Pensive Poet

Dr Rajashree A N

BookLeaf Publishing

India | USA | UK

Made with ❤ on the BookLeaf Publishing Platform
www.bookleafpub.in
www.bookleafpub.com

Dedication

I dedicate this book to my readers and to those
ephemeral moments when life seems to unravel itself.

Preface

This poetry collection is a culmination of musings on diverse emotions that we go through at some point in life. Every turn of page is a narrative which takes you on a roller coaster, from depths of despair to heights of happiness. The poems are, fables of fighters foraging on inner demons, anecdotes on love, ballads on bliss of motherhood and personifications of the most abstract thoughts. Each poem will leave you room for reflection. So I hope you sit back and enjoy the ride.

Acknowledgements

My eternal gratitude

To my Mother, the light of my life, the pillar of my world, for her glowing wisdom & virtues lighting my path, for her unwavering support and unconditional love. For being the best role model I could ever ask for. For always believing in me. My strength & aspirations stem from her.

To my Father, my protector, for his shining intellect is my inspiration. For his love & forever encouraging me, all through my baby steps to giant leaps, while having my back whenever I stumbled.

To my Uncles, for cherishing my existence, for being my rock & for their immeasurable support.

To my Husband, my world, for his love and for being the wind beneath my wings.

Covid: reflections

HOLD ON

The contagium reduced
the future to a wraith
Yet you thrive on
Hope and Faith
Embracing your scars
You pick up your broken self
Dreaming of blue sky
Hold on to your sails
The Sun always smiles
Above the gloomy clouds
Beyond the angry storms
So let the stars be the witness
Let the moon sing a lullaby
That once was a being
Who walked the dark path
And all the way to light

DO YOU CARE?

Donned in PPE lands the angel in white
He saves the gasping souls and how!
He is their one and only light
Do you care about his religion now?

Donned in PPE arrives the white knight
To rescue the sick off their breathless plight
He is their only soldier in their dreadful fight!
Do you care if he is black or white?

Donned in PPE appears the healer, **THE ONE** in white
with none to the left or to the right
To heal, the ailing wailing clutching a talisman
Do you care if **THE ONE** is a man or a woman?

SEIZE THE DAY

I sit on a chair
At the wall I stare
Not knowing at all
What's gonna befall

Will I make it through this wave
This pandemic will it take me away
Tonight in hell will I dine
Your guess is as good as mine

So I shake my head
for enough I've had
I say I am done
and decide to abandon
this fear of doomsday
And I get up
to seize the day

Westerly

I sang along the westerly wind
ballads of spring and untimely fling
Grazed my skin thy ravenous breeze
my brazen eyes are such a tease

Swept me away my westerly wind
I no longer dance to worldly whim
Blown away in your golden glints
Thy monsoon bathed my mortal sins

I reminisce our tango oh westerly wind
We soared in the azure in a whirlwind
I wished to sail on waves of blue
And you blew and blew and blew

Inner light

Thrown off vaporous glory
Your soul floated like a lone cloud
Squeezing your soul off its misery
You set the cloud as your sail
Yet you sailed unaware
And I gazed in a daze

When the storms of sorrow arose
In your mind's tranquil ocean
You let the pearls of peace cast ashore
Yet you smiled unaware
At day's scarlet face

And in the pitch-black of the night
when darkness enveloped you
You, the wonder of aurora's light
I got to witness with my star-struck eyes
The incandescent light of your own
And in your light the stars shone

LowRise

It's been some time
Life feels like a gunny sack
filled with stones strapped on my back
Dragging it along my every step
My back arching and aching
My shoulders stiff and cramping
A pleasant morning for the world
But the sun is glaring at me
blinding me, restraining me
While I strive in pursuit of excellence
Mediocrity has quietly made a mansion out of my life

But It's time!
For a herculean renovation
To empty that hefty sack of preclusion
Rip up the straight jacket and scream aloud
Defy the dictum and fly above the cloud
Hold those unpropitious hues of blue and black
and just paint like Vincent Van Gogh
Behold oh Destiny

If you are high, I am your highness
I will burn your malevolence and rise from its ashes
And I rise and I rise, I RISE

New Sunrise

I wept under the sorrows of the sky
As the sun never beamed his smile
Stars hid behind the ebony tile
And the moon faded into a new lie
So let me sleep through
this anguish for now
I know not
what tomorrow brings along
Across the wall of my dreamscape
a river sings a soporific song
Let me sleep through my silent cries
After every sunset lies a new sunrise
When I wake up and go through it all
And make my mark before the last petal's fall

I hang on

Dark shroud
Inexplicable pain
numbing brain
Who is to be blamed
What's left to be reclaimed
What's sane? am I insane?
For I smile I laugh
While I cry and die inside
No sight of any respite
to this reiterating bane
As shame precludes me
from seeking my family
Emptiness has me blind
as I see no friend
Just one step away
to make it all go away
As tempting as it seems
Every single day
I choose
To never give up on me

Even when I have lost
all controls over me
I muster up strength
just enough To choose
Life over death
Every single day
I gather enough breath
to speak to my kith
and to my kin
It's not a sin
even if I bare it to an alien
My mind unable to think
hence I listen to my shrink
I pop his pill
It saves me from
falling off the hill
What ever works
I do it all
to evade the fall
into the depths of depression
I am hanging by the cliff
with my nails
As tempting as it may be
To let go and peace be
But I hang on
Every single day
Till the sun rises behind the cliff

And the dark shroud clears away

The Chase

Let's hold our hands together
and chase the Northern Lights
Let's see the cosmic ballet
under the starry nights

Let's brave this chilly air
burning the fire of ambition inside
Let's scale these snowy hills with flair
leaving behind the world outside

Let's sail on a boat of grit
seeking the celestial spectacle all lit
Let's forge in fanatic fervour
soaking in Aurora in myriad of colour

Togetherness, nurture and adventure
that's the heart of the matter
Let's clad us in warm embrace
and marvel at dance, what grace!

The night is clear and we are here
With North Pole at sight
Let's hold our hands together
and chase the Northern Lights
Let's see the cosmic ballet
under the starry nights

My First Ray of Light

The twinkle in your eyes
endearing innocent smile
love springs inside of me
pure and unseen erstwhile

Those tiny feet and fingers
caressing my soul
In your colourful babbles
and honey dipped giggles
I rest assured

Your mischievous grins
and every impish ploy
to draw my attention
fills my life with riotous joy

Clinging to my leg
like a koala cub
your angelic face
restores my faith in humanity

With your tender little arms
hugging my fears
I could live on for eternity

Pointless Pursuit

Day in and day out
Rushing in and dashing out
In this mad pace
All that rat race

It's a random bus ride
A ticket to nowhere
That express drive
Heading for, God knows where !
Helter-skelter everywhere

Drowning in a lucid trance
Swayed in to a conscious Daze
Snap me out of this tricker
Stop me trailing the Pied Piper

Together

Together we seek
the wonders of this world
We marvel at silver alps
revel in cosmic lights
and gape in disbelief
at Khufu's rocks

Together we fly
in the solitude skies
Lost in each other's
galactic gaze
we float on fluffs
of vanilla pouffe
in yonder cafe au lait
where the vermilion melts
on cerulean waves
And Luna draws coyly
an ebony veil of haze

Cobblestone Streets of Praha

Walking down the cobblestone streets
I walk into a time, the stories are made of
When the ground was clacking of hoofbeats
High hats, long tail coats, men carried off

Meandering lanes as I follow
My senses are lured by, Rococo
Avenues filled with heady Aromas
of cinnamon caramel Trdlo,
Impeccably lined with edifices
In shades of pastel high and low

The Saints blessing the Stone Bridge
Hovering the cerulean Vltava
Whispering Hymn into my ears
Like a cooing hum of a partridge
Archaic Legends of bygone years

Gazing across the Skyline so spiky
At the gates of Namesti Republiky
Spellbinding sights of steeples
As Hundreds of spires pierce the sky
With those religious needles

The Petrin Hill bathing in morning dew
Is worthy of thousands of footsteps
As Summit, seeped in splendid view
Of Tangerine tiled rooftops
Draping the Strana in golden hue

Enchanted beyond words can say,
Finding myself in the Hallway,
of the most Bewitching Castle
I twirl and dance
Not a St.Vitus dance!
The breathtaking namesake Cathedral

As I tread these stony streets,
once trodden by kafka
Dim-lit lamps gracing the streets,
cast a glow of ochre
Frozen in time this Bohemian Town
I yearn to explore more and more,

But then it was time
the clock struck nine
That Mystical clock of the Old Town

Had been a while since I fell in love,
with a city at first sight
I fell in love while Walking down the
Cobblestone Streets of Praha

Dear Heart

My melancholic little heart
How many more sorrows do you want
Beyond your four chambers can contain

Guess what!
Felicity has taken a token
and waiting in line, in anticipation!
Along with some others
Joy, Merry and Cheers.
Isn't it high time
for your stiff Valves to open
and let in those pretty happiness?

You pair with pathos
Like cheese and wine?
If that's how you feel, it's not fine!
Have you ever tried 'Amore'?
It tastes better, an ideal entrée
It does age well with time
And That, is your red wine

I know that Regret
Has long been your Rhythm
But at this Rate
I tell you, You will never fathom
the strength of Forgiveness, Honey!
You will cease to Beat in Synchrony

My dear Rouge, you are blushing blue
As Heaviness is weighing you down
Now don't you frown, I won't let you down
Just shed your Blight, and reclaim your Health!
Well, may be you are set in your ways
But it's Now! to Reset the Waves
of your holy Lifeline

Best Gift

My Best gift ever
arrived unplanned
The gift, most precious,
was laid into my hand

Wrapped in a bundle
A sight to enjoy
Your coos and gurgles
gave oodles of joy

I went on with life
ever without a map
Until the day
you came into my lap

You gave me strength
to face any storm
The moment when
You called me mom

So Wherever you go
Whatever you do
My child, in my heart
I'll always have you

Arise

I peer into my foggy soul in mutiny
Hundred lifetimes made me colder
I invoke my abysmal fire
Let my spirit emblaze my destiny

Like a seafarer, lone resilient
Set on horizonal goal
In the essence of the present
shall glide my unconquerable soul

Like an albatross soaring over
Who seldom flies straight
It could very well be much older
Let my ship roll in its trait

When the hourglass runs out of sand
Peace reigns upon this chime
And the heavens duly embrace
What the earth could barely stand

Haiku

FROZEN

Frozen lake mirrors
A frozen smile on my face
Seeks apricity

LAST FLICKER

Hanging by twilight
Dawn of the night brings cold air
Light escapes my soul

WINTER

Frosty leaves glimmer
in the scent of icy air
when winter blossoms

WARMTH OF NOSTALGIA

Dulcet robin sings
on snowy bush of holly
Sunny nostalgia

One Day...

One day these floors
will not be flooded with toys
One day these giggles
will no longer drown the halls

Those tiny hands
playing with my face,
will find their own wings
and fly somewhere else

When you leave my nest to make
one of your own my child,
your childhood plays I'll rake
in the tree house where you used to hide

One day my heart
will miss u in umpteen ways
Until then I'll make a note
of your sweet innocent ways

Let me hug you one more time
Read stories to you at bedtime
Make your favourite s'more
Build castles with you on the shore

I shall cheer as you slide
And push you on a high swing
As tomorrow these games are
the memories to cling

Let's draw some paper art
Stick some glitters on glue
I want to be a part
Of every little thing you do

Until you learn to tie on your own
Allow me to tie your shoes
Until you learn to walk alone
Let me carry you like kangaroos

So Let me wash your hair
For now help you climb the stair
My son, when you are all grown
Remember all the love that was shown

The Irony

In the depth of darkness found the rays of
enlightenment,
For the darkest hour revealed the truest colour.

The power of knowledge embrittled the ego,
For it weakened the lies, enfeebled the fears.

The webs of cognisance detangled the doubts,
For the specks of insights decluttered the mind.

The winds of change blew the delusion away,
For the change was only a mirage, the core prevailed.

The vision of the future blinded the past,
For the clarity of purpose blurred the distant distress.

The illness of the body healed the mind to health,
The languishing pain bore a joyous new birth,
And in the war of the self,
dawned peace to the soul solace to the heart.

Woken

Lost in the lyrical life
I ceased to sing my song
Aimlessly I wandered seeking
the Orient light all along

Dew glistened in dawn's light
Scattered my morning haze
Wind woke my vapid heart
to the melody of cyan waves

Night lit up with fireflies
Woke my soul to see
Just like a new butterfly
that was trapped is now free

Short Poems

Mother

Every time I peer into
Your Soul so Pure and Innocent
It Swells my heart and my eyes
Well up with tears flowing down
For I am touched by divinity
As its You wherein
I see the God exist

Celestial

Perched atop a hill at dawn
I caught a glimpse of night depart
clad in cobalt kimono
When the stars summoned the cosmos
to shine their empyrean abode
Spellbound, I gaped at magic unfold
As the sky was steeped in moon's silver

While the sun was colouring it gold

Dawn

As the Sol ascends at dawn
The sky turns into a canvas
With strokes of palette
In gold and scarlet

Ode to the fallen

Waves whisper to the stars
Above the taciturn sea
Tales of the trepid tears
Buried beneath the sea

Wind carries the echoes
Of promises drowned and lost
Whirls of wretched sigh of woes
As the moon glistened with frost

Hiss

Every night
As I turn off my bedside light
I close my eyes and turn to a side
A chilly mist engulfs me in a cocoon
And a wheezy voice whispers
"I'm coming for you soon"

Emerald

Flowers of doom
in Withering sorrow
cry crimson tears
And curse the land
before they perish
along with roots
entwining the sphere
Thus the emerald paradise
is lost for manifold years

Play

While I was busy seeking Life
that didn't look bleak
Life was peeping at me
playing hide and seek

Billet doux

I search for my star
In the galaxy of your eyes
Let me catch your whispers
Falling from my sighs
Steal my silence
And weave it into your song
Hide my name in your heart
And beat for me strong

Orchid

Blessed be the dove
With emotions so torrid
You bathe our love
Like rain-kissed orchid

Our love isn't a purple fantasy
Nor a lilac lie
It isn't for the faint-heart to fancy
But an ode to a fervent sky

If

If I let you see my tears
Would you show me your pain
Drowning all of our fears
Would you hug me under the rain

Picturesque

Mountains pierce the sky
Clouds chase the sun
Sun dips into the sea
Stars come out of hiding

A politician's musing-Limerick

It's so rare to find a citizen sublime
In this world filled with grime and slime
That when I find one
I intend to retain the one
Locked up for the longest of the time

Clandestine

Soot from my heart burning of desire
Formed the kohl of my eyes
And you fell for my smoky eyes
That singed your surreptitious soul

Despondent

Nimbus cloud looms over
a blotchy pale
lazuli sky of my heart
Heart's roots are grapevines
Burrowing through my sanguine veins
Into the vineyard of my mind
Where the skeletons of forgotten wishes
hang alongside half moth-eaten
monochrome photos of regrets
With empty kernels of residual time

On the line

Life hangs on the line
Like the clothes on the washing line
Flapping in the winds of time
Up and down the peaks and troughs
of the Lifeline
As the wind ceases to blow
so does Life,
still and motionless,
falling on flatline

Nan's

Waves knocked on the seashore
with delicate flowers of foam
Always left at the beach door
The place I called my home

Brine breezed into my skin pore
I saw the hermits roam
Pretty Seashells washed ashore
and once I found a gnome

Childhood memories I explore
of sea, sand and humid gloam
Tidal pools of colours outpour
Lookin' at nan's pic in monochrome

That's all they need

Let it sink into your mind
In a life under the sun
All you need to be is kind
Heart weighs a ton

You'll see if you look around
from the eyes of your soul
That we lost more than found
This world in a rice bowl

Yet, To be held in love
is hard to find indeed
Teach the kids to love
that's all they need

www.ingramcontent.com/pod-product-compliance
Lightning Source LLC
Chambersburg PA
CBHW070609160726
48003CB00005B/2187